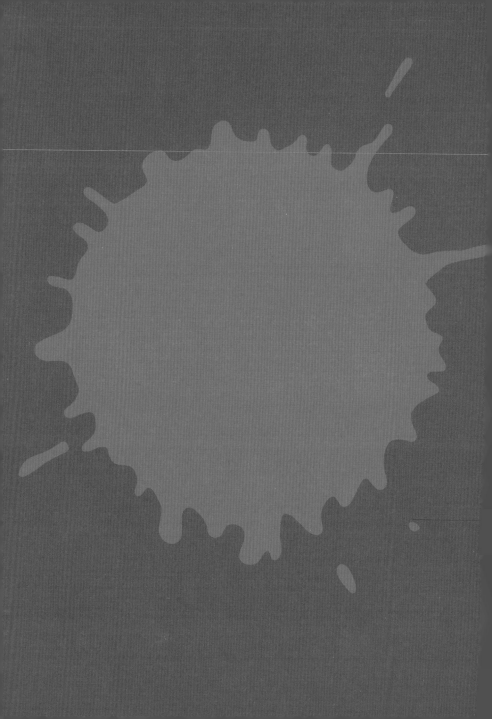

DID YOU KNOW?
Red Panda

DID YOU KNOW?

Red Panda

young
reed

Contents

Red Panda facts

- The Red Panda is an arboreal mammal, meaning that it spends much of its life in trees.

- They are about the size of a large pet cat.

● Red Pandas sleep for up to **sixteen hours** per day, often slung along a tree branch.

● Another name for the species is the **Lesser Panda**.

Special adaptations

- Red Pandas are **nocturnal** – they can see well in the dark and are active mostly at night

- Their white face patterns help mums and babies to **see each other in the dark.**

- They sleep with their **tail** wrapped around their head to keep warm.

- Unusually, each Red Panda paw has **six digits** to help them climb trees.

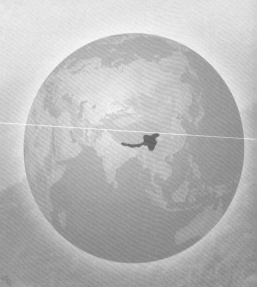

Where do they live?

● Today, captive Red Pandas are a familiar sight in **zoos** and **animal parks** around the world, where they have become a favourite attraction for millions of people.

● In the wild, however, Red Pandas live only in **high-altitude forests** in Asia, in parts of India, Nepal, Bhutan, Myanmar and China.

Red Panda.

Closest relatives

● The Red Panda's scientific name is *Ailurus fulgens*, which means **'fire-coloured cat'**.

● It is not closely related to cats — it is such a **unique animal** that it is placed in a family all on its own.

● Of other animals alive today, **skunks** and **racoons** are thought to be the Red Panda's closest relatives.

Racoon.

Skunk.

Red Panda.

The 'other' panda

● Although both animals eat bamboo and have a similar-looking pale furry face with dark patches over the eyes, the Red Panda is **not** closely **related** to the **Giant Panda**.

● The 1.5-metre-long Giant Panda is a **vegetarian bear** that like its namesake specialises in a diet of bamboo.

● It lives only in a few **mountain forests** in **central China.**

Giant Panda.

Territory matters

- Each Red Panda has a territory covering about **one square kilometre** of forest.

- They usually live **alone**, except when breeding.

- Red Pandas live in trees, using their **long bushy tails** for balance.

- Long retractable **claws** help them to cling on to trunks and branches and climb through the forest.

What's for dinner?

- **Ninety-eight per cent** of a Red Panda's food is **bamboo**.

- They can only **digest** about a quarter of the food they eat, so they have to eat a lot to survive.

- Red Pandas eat up to **twenty thousand** bamboo leaves **every day**.

- With all the undigested leaves, they produce a lot of **poo!**

Mother Red Panda with baby.
(Rainer Halama/Wikimedia Commons)

Family life

● Baby Red Pandas are born in a **den** in a hollow in a tree trunk or among rocks.

● They are born with fur but blind, and rely on their **mother's milk** for the first few months of life.

● The young, known as **cubs**, are fully grown after **one year**.

Threats to Red Pandas

- Red Pandas are considered **Endangered** – in 2024 it was estimated that there may only be **2,500** left in the wild.

- Their population is **declining** and they are threatened by losing their homes to **deforestation**.

- Other problems include **climate change** affecting their habitat and food supply.

First published in 2025 by
New Holland Publishers
Sydney

newhollandpublishers.com

Level 1, 178 Fox Valley Road, Wahroonga, NSW 2076, Australia

A record of this book is held at the National Library of Australia.

ISBN 978 1 92107 391 5

OTHER TITLES IN THE 'DID YOU KNOW?' SERIES:

Kangaroos
ISBN 978 1 92107 386 1

Koala
ISBN 978 1 92107 387 8

Lizards
ISBN 978 1 92107 388 5

Penguins
ISBN 978 1 92107 390 8

Meerkat
ISBN 978 1 92107 389 2

For details of these books and hundreds
of other Natural History titles see
newhollandpublishers.com